Management styles, management techniques and management methods learned easily

Ronny Behr

Texts: © Copyright by

Ronny Behr Rottwerndorfer Str. 44
01257 Dresden
info@ronnybehr.de

All rights reserved. All rights of the work lie with the author.

Translation: Romy Rimkus

Prologue

You can find several books and articles about management techniques respectively leadership of employees in the Internet. I have read a lot of these books. However, even more valuable were the experiences I acquired during my work as a manager.
With this small book I would like to share my knowledge and my experiences regarding management styles and management techniques in a compressed way.

I suggest that you should read this book to the fullest to understand it content wise. Afterwards you can take notes while going through the book again. The most important thing is the usage in the field. Feel free to test the different management styles and techniques.

Index

- Management work is mental work
- Description and definition of management styles
- Management styles
  - Authoritarian leadership
  - Example for authoritarian leadership
  - Laissez-faire leadership
  - Cooperative leadership
  - Situational leadership
- Transactional leadership
  - Management by – summary
- Transformational leadership
  - Meaning of transformational leadership
  - Usage of transformational leadership
- Synopsis

Management work is mental work

In this book you get to see an overview of management styles. You will learn which management styles do exist and how you can adapt them into your daily work. The most important management styles will be detailed and accentuated with examples. This combination of theory and practice shall help you to access this topic easily. This book does not demand for integrity but for learnable techniques that you can apply immediately.

As a team leader, supervisor, manager, department manager or line manager you are an executive. Alongside several social skills you ought to know and master specific management styles and techniques.

Whilst the butcher needs to master the cooking of the sausages and a mechanic needs to cut metal, you, as an executive, need management styles and methods. The special methods include several techniques about leading employees and employee motivation. Besides several other instruments, the knowledge of the above-mentioned terms is essential for your daily work. By this I mean exactly what I am writing.

I once attended training about management styles and techniques. A colleague of mine rated it with 'nice to know' but just theory. That was not the interest that was needed for this topic, at least in my opinion.
If someone does not know management styles, will never be able to lead situationally. That means he will never be able to change his management style wittingly and correctly. Nevertheless for me, this consciousness makes the fine difference between a leader and a good leader. Only if you succeed, by the help of special techniques, to adjust yourself to your opponent

you will be on the same wavelength.

The work of a leader has a lot to do with mental work. That is the reason why executives are mostly paid better than "normal" colleagues. You bear more responsibility and you are always right in the middle of everything. The pressure from above and beneath comes on a regular basis.

To deal with the pressure you can use these management methods to influence your employees and to organise your work and their work usefully. Organise the work does not mean that you have to or need to set everything for them. You need to see yourself as a guiding instance. You give inspiration and motivation to your employees. You don't even need more knowledge than them. You only need to know rough details and most of all you need to know who suits the task to be solved the most.

DESCRIPTION AND DEFINITION OF MANAGEMENT STYLES

In the following I will go into the term of management styles. A definition of this term shall help you develop a essential understanding of it. I will address management methods but I will not list all of the known ones. I am concentrating on methods which have proved to be successful and that are suiting my favoured management style. Why do I do that? It is because I know that it will work and I want you to have usable knowledge by the end of the day.

Do you already know some management styles? Basically management styles are a repeating pattern of actions in regard of your own work. To learn which management style you are using you can take one of the numerous tests in the internet. Please, always see these tests as an indicator not as a cat's whiskers. This is really important. Such a test can only show you a frame, nothing more. Better rely on yourself.

Management styles can be seen from different perspectives. At one point you can look at the management style itself. Then you can look at the dimension, also with the background of special dialogical advantages or from the point of an exchange relationship between employee and superior. You also can only look at the direction respectively the current most important alignment.

A lot of theory regarding management styles exists. Many decades a lot of different personalities have dealt with this topic. There are a vast number of classification and explanation.

You already notice that it is all very vague, theoretical and complex. Therefore I try to simplify everything for you. You should get something tangible out of this book. Therefore the classification of management styles is provided in a practical and comprehensible way.

MANAGEMENT STYLES

Very common and especially for beginners well suited are the following views respectively distinctions of management styles.

Authoritarian management style

With this management style there is little to none leeway for your employees. You call the shots. You are making all the decisions on the basis of existing information. You punish contraventions or denials. Attention: Punishment does not mean corporal punishment. A punishment could for example be a warning or a serious employee appraisal. This management style is very common respectively comes standard within army units. A Clear advantage and also feature of this management style is the high decision and execution speed.

Example for an authoritarian management style

A good example for an authoritarian management style is a fire alert. How many people are really familiar with every process regarding the rescue of employees verbatim? As most of the people don't know every procedure it's the same for me myself. I have read all of that at some time or another and also looked at an evacuation plan which is displayed in the company. Once the alert started screaming I got up and gave proper and short instructions. 'Everything stays in its place.' I shouted out loud so everyone on the huge area could hear me for sure. In the hallway you could already hear commotion. In front of the staircase was a knot of people and the door that led to the staircase was very small. There was only enough space so that one to two people could pass through and naturally you are not that fast on a staircase as you are on a ground-levelled street.

I've stood in the middle of the crowd, raised my arms and called 'Everyone takes the emergency door behind me!' Thereby I led the stream into the right direction. Most of them didn't even know the emergency exit until now. Furthermore were most of the people put off by the alert protection that was installed on the door. They didn't want to do something wrong.

Now everyone was running past me on the right and left side. It felt like I was standing in the middle of a river. Suddenly the staircase was empty again and the group began to move. In what felt like a minute, everyone was outside. On this exercise more than 100 of people had left the alleged danger zone swift and organized. . Despite the fact that I didn't read the entire process again. I had only taken the lead.

Short and glassy statements should be a form of authority.

Not only emergencies require an authoritarian management style. Especially new hired employees would be totally overwhelmed if you would always ask what they want to do next. New employees don't know the company. They don't know anything about processes, they are not familiar with the new work and they don't know their new colleagues as well.

This is where a straight leadership with straight demands is needed. Authority does not mean impolite. I know most people associate impoliteness with an authoritarian management style. This assumption is incorrect. In this connection it just means that you call the shots.
Without deviation but willingly with a friendly smile and accentuated with an offer to help. Finishing this with a short real-life example:

"Mr. Meyer, please compile the report for the sales figures of the last week until tomorrow 9 am for me. The report should be a PDF file and should not contain more than two pages. Do you need anything more information from me? ... No? Fine. We Will meet tomorrow morning at 9 am in my office.

This instruction states clearly what to do (PDF file, not more than 2 pages). The timeline is included, even twice. This is a so-called repeater. Tomorrow there will be no " I forgot it" or "I overheard it". The place of the handover defined and in the end, the employee had the chance to get help.

LAISSEZ-FAIRE MANAGEMENT STYLE

This is the management style with the most disadvantages, at least in my opinion. Why? The employees have all the freedom in the world. They are making all decisions on their own and the manager, in this case you, will not intervene. For companies, which place high priority on creativity, could it be a reasonable management style. With a laissez-faire management style the mayhem may be pre-programmed, but purposely.

It could be possible that a contention arises within the group of employees. It could contain topics like who calls the shots the most or which employee can do this or that the best. It is also possible that the discipline will suffer. As a manager you only set the expected result, more or less. You can use this style when it comes to voluntary work. This could be in form of planning a team event. In this case it makes sense to not exert too much pressure on the employees.

Example for a Laissez-faire management style

"Mr. Meyer we would like to hold a company festivity next month. A lot of colleagues have told me that you are always very committed. Would you like to organise the event? I'll give you free rein with that. Nevertheless be aware that the budget of EUR 3,000 should not be exceeded. When shall I expect your ideas?"

To be honest, the example is still very guiding, but it is the result that counts. In the example the employee gets motivated through positive feedback of a third party. The only thing that counts is the fact that he will take on the assignment voluntarily and with pleasure. The rest lies literally in his hands. Another, yet wittingly excessive example for a team:

"Hello everybody, there you have a room, a flipchart and a lot of pens. Do what you want with all of that. The most important thing is, by the end of the day, you have designed a new product."

In this example there is no lead at all, at least not from my perspective. It is most likely that there will be a leader in this group sooner or later. That is part of every normal group-dynamic process. In my opinion, I give any type of leadership directly into the group. Without holding any control.

CO-OPERATIVE MANAGEMENT STYLE

Applying this management style your employees are fully integrated. Some also call this management style democratic leadership. Democratic is not so much the issue here. Your subordinates could and should participate actively. Standards and targets are set together. Everyone has a say. The most important thing is: The decisions are still made by you. That's the reason why the word democracy is inappropriate.

An important characteristic of the co-operative management style is transparency. With a high transparency it is easier for all to understand processes and decisions. A major disadvantage is the related low decision speed. Through an early and deep integration of your employees you will always achieve a high motivation and engagement among your employees.

At first sight, it seems difficult to apply a co-operative management style in most branches, but there are ways and means to do it anyway.

In an employee appraisal you can agree on this or that target with your employee. You can give him alternatives so he can choose for himself. You are co-operative. Important is that the possible alternative is given by you. An example from a call centre:

"Mr. Meyer, we have now looked at the progress of the last weeks together. On what shall we work together for next weeks? On your customer satisfaction values or your call receipt speed?

Both possibilities are extremely important key figures in a call center. Since both figures have potential, you can take advantage of that circumstance and give your employee the idea of having the choice. This, of course, can be applied on any other branch.

Situational management style

Basically this is not a management style anymore, but rather a method. I have integrated it in the previous order on purpose, to highlight the importance of that paragraph.

Situational leadership means that you combine every known management style depending on the situation and you are applying them according to the type of situation or employee. For this purpose you have already read examples. For the fire drill I have adapted myself to the situation and I've changed into the authoritarian management style.

The authoritarian management style is also useful with new employees. When it comes to a common evening with the team I use the Laissez-faire management style. In the daily business I often use a combination of the co-operative and authoritarian management style.

From now on you should consider briefly which management style suits the current moment the best. In case of the delay of an employee you should always use an authoritarian management style. The same also applies for team training.

For a quality circle, which has the target of finding improvements, you should better use the co-operative management style.

For the monthly performance review it is appropriate to use the co-operative management style. Just imagine possible situations, maybe on your way to work, and consider which management style suits it best.

Being forward-thinking lets you choose the right management style in the end. The most important thing is that you imagine those situations visually or auditory. Therefore you really hear or see them. This will ensure that you can later refer to situations you already experienced and that you can benefit from them.

Even if they are not real, your brain has created a pattern of thinking out of them. You will therefore succeed better in choosing the right way during the right moment.

Maybe you've already heard of gut feeling. That is exactly what we are talking about, in that case.

Transactional Leadership

Well, now you know the most important views and the situation-related usage, we should enrich your management style with even more methods. Transactional leadership means leading with a give and take. The employee gives you a specific performance and you will give him something back. Transactional leadership often is associated with the Mb-concepts.

Maybe you have already heard of those "Management by..." concepts. The most used concept may be Management by Objectives. Known are at least eight "Management by..." concepts.

Management by - Summary

Management by Crisis means the (intentionally) cause of crisis and

emergency situations to increase the performance of the employees, because of a specific emotional condition. This concept is really marginal, because a conscious constructed crises could definitely become a real crisis.
Furthermore you could accuse this management style of unethical intentions.
It is quite conceivable that there exists a connection to a possible enemy image.

Example for an artificial constructed "crisis":

The other department, the competitor or anyone could be such an image of an enemy.

If the "others" would win the challenge, we are not allowed to participate in the company outing.

Management by Systems is based on the teaching of control circuits, the cybernetics. There are several self-controlling units within this control circuit. These get their tasks from the management (Management by Delegation). Ongoing control and response (Management by Results) causes appropriate reactions respectively an intervention by the management (Management by Exception).

So with this, this concept is a mixture of many "Management by …" concepts. For this book definitely a way to theoretical approach. It might be a right one, but I don't want to confuse you, but I want to show you tangible examples and methods.

Management by Results is a concept, which has little to do with trust. The targets are, other than by management by Objectives, given by the management. There is no deviation from these numbers, which leads to some sort of fanaticism of numbers in some extent.

This concept only works with permanent control of all employees respectively units. In my opinion this concept only works partially and usually just for a definite period of time.

The application of this concept is conceivable based on Management by Crisis or in relation of Change Management. With a permanent use of these concepts a exceptionally high fluctuation and an increasing sickness rate is expected.

Management by Decision Rules means that every employee has an extremely heavy manual with him respectively has memorised everything from it and applies every single rule in there, in every detail and without exception.
This sentence was not really gallantly phrased, but it suits it best. This concept tends to be really bureaucratically and this means that it hardly has any motivating effect.

In this concept creativity is more or less suppressed by nearly 100 %. This means that the unit respectively the team cannot develop. The development has to happen from the outside. If the management misses this a standstill, frustration and strong operational blindness will occur.

Management by Delegation only means that the management distributes and transfers tasks further in accordance to ones abilities.
Some might say "Ah, this concept my boss also applies..." however, it probably isn't like that.

As a manager you are forced to transfer one or another task to someone else anyway. This has nothing to do with this concept directly, but it is basically the task of a manager.

Management by Delegation is really static, because it has specific general conditions. These are, for example, the existing job descriptions. These are fixing the frame for the things that could and should be transferred. Management by Delegation is also applied in the Federal Armed Forces. The platoon leader gives the radio command to the radio operator and the command to drive to the driver. If the radio operator also has a driving license is beyond any discussion.

Management by Exception
means that the manager intervenes in exceptional cases. The target of this concept is the discharge of management. Only if the employee reaches a specific limit respectively a specific value, the manager intervenes. Until that employees can decide and design their work for themselves. It is distinguished into two versions, active and passive.

By using the active version the manager intervenes if he things that it's necessary.

By using the passive version the manager only intervenes if the employee asks for it or if some targets will not be achieved.

The discharge of the manager can definitely be an enrichment. The difficulty with this concept is the exception threshold. If it's defined incorrectly, catastrophically effects could happen.

It is best to imagine a garden barrel. If it's full it's going to overflow. If you install a float with a signalling device, that only reacts when the barrel is full, you will always have the water in the garden. It's better to let the float react at a filling quantity of 90 %.

Management by Walking around is not an actual management method, but a communication instrument. Some other sources name this concept Management by Wandering around.

The approach of Mbwa is to get the manager out of his office. Instead of hiding behind the monitor of his computer the boss gets the chance to speak to his employees directly.

This, of course, avoids the amount of misunderstandings and decreases the email communication substantially.

The manager also gets a quick and intensive feeling of what's important for the employees right now. Ideally the manager plans a small time slot on a daily base and to just go for a "round". This concept works even better, if the manager approaches the employee with a specific target. This could be, for example, providing the employee with information. This could happen out of different reasons.

Management by Projects means the coordination, planning, controlling and monitoring of projects, even over different departments. If the target is achieved and/or the task is done, the project also ends. For you as a manager it is quite conceivable, if you devide your team into two groups and let them work on a task.

Management by Objectives

means leading employees through an agreement of (similar) targets. Nowadays this method is applied quite often. The targets are often generated on the base of S.M.A.R.T. MbO is a method which could be assigned to transactional management on the base of work-psychological aspects.

This management style is based on some kind of exchange between the manager and his employee. This means, that the employee gets targets through the agreement, which he has to fulfil. In the case of fulfilment the employee gets a reward in the form of material or immaterial benefits.

In case of non-fulfilment the employee gets an appropriate feedback or sanctions. For this purpose I want to give you an example from my call centre experience.

Mr. Meier did his work very well within the last weeks. His quality values increased and all of his calls sounded really professional.

Nonetheless, the quality assessment didn't comply with what you expected while hearing his calls. The long talking times were criticised by his callers. Contrary to the general opinion of call centre agents that a long call increases their quality, the customers see it from a complete other point of view. I met up with Mr. Meier for a short exchange.

The meeting had the character of an employee appraisal. For me it was more of a coaching.
We talked about different facets of his calls and listened to some records. It turned out that the normal caller calls us, because he wanted a quick solution for his problem.

Emphasis is placed on quick. Somehow it is quite logical. If you put yourself in the position of the caller it occurs, that oneself has no desire to hold long telephone calls with an employee of a hotline after a long working day.

Mr. Meier also found this out for himself. Despite this self-awareness I wanted to reward his effort in some special way.

In our position as a team manager we were able to assign special skills to the employees.
"Skill" is a term that is often used in the call centre for special abilities. The employee gets more competencies and gets qualified for more tasks after attending a training.

As managers we were close to our employees and we could evaluate the performance and commitment the best. I knew that Mr. Meier had a good mind to process the incoming emails. Therefore we agreed on a worthwhile target.

Mr. Meier had to reduce his call time sustainably by 130 seconds within a few weeks. If he succeeded he would get an email training from me and after that would be able to process emails.

Mr. Meier was more than excited. On the one hand he knew that it was important to give a quick service and on the other hand he got a reward from me besides the general recognition of the customer. Mr. Meier achieved the target with ease.

With this, my management style in this situation (situational management) complied with the classical transactional management.
I got the "better" call time and Mr. Meier got his email skill.

On closer inspection something specific is noted. It was not only about the expansion of abilities respectively about a normal exchange. It has happened more.

Thereby, we get to another management style, the transformational management style. This style is an extension of transactional management. It is not only about giving and taking anymore.

Transformational management is about a greater and common (company) target. I easily could have focused on a simple upskilling, but by taking my time for Mr. Meier and by playing his record calls to him, he recognised the meaning of the target of a reduced call time.

Practically by himself, because he was highly motivated, he dealt with his task with flying colours and he also achieved his target and mine with ease.

Transformational Leadership

At the moment there is only little known about this style. When researching the topic transformational management style, you will mostly find some studies and theses, which are dealing with evidence and success stories. All of them have one thing in common: They prove that this management style is even more successful than any other.

You won't find many appropriate methods regarding transformational leadership. When I first read about this style, I spent a lot of time on it and tried a lot. In the process some really important things emerged within.

Meaning of transformational leadership

Transformational leadership means that the manager is aware of common management styles and methods. That is indeed one of the most important points. Furthermore, the manager knows every single team member very well. This includes, besides technical knowledge, some private details as well. It's the person behind the work who matters in the first place.

The aim of transformational leader ship is to change the awareness and attitude of an employee towards his work. To transform.

This management style requires that the employees accept their supervisor as their leader consistently. With leader I did not mean the leader hierarchically but as the only possible and wanted option.

In many documents there is talk that a transformational manager seems extremely charismatic to its employees. The employees are extraordinarily loyal towards their leader. You could almost say that they are doing their work out of courtesy exceptionally good.

In summary it can be said, therefore, that transformational management means the following:

Being a role model and to build trust to gain loyalty (idealized influence). This means that a transformational leading manager participates as well. He shouldn't be timid about mucking in. Independent of the branch, every manager can hitch up their knickers and give their employees a hand.

Furthermore it involves motivating the employees with challenging and sensible targets and because of that to increase their motivation (inspirational motivation). Setting a target only because of the target will not advance the company. The employee has no incentive and will get bored easily. The manager has in fact done "something", but it will not last for long. Therefore, an agreed target has to be challenging.

Stimulate independency and creativity (intellectual stimulation). This also means to participate amongst other things. It even more means to show how it should be done. Show your employees what you are able to do and challenge them to participate. Rise to a challenge together with your employees. Demand new ideas for improvement.

Promote employees individually, so that they can evolve their own skills and strengths (individualized consideration). Don't set the same targets with every employee and avoid templates! Respond to every employee individually. Observe his strengths, but mostly, ask for his professional preferences.

Combine your Observations with the results of your interview. For example, when you observe that your employee is reading an excel book during his lunch break and that he told you that he likes to program macros, let him create a reporting once in a while. At first assign an easy reporting to him and later let him create some dodgy ones.

Only with your advancement your employee will experience an appreciation and can reach his wish even more. After all he needs material to practice. If he is good in what he is doing he may optimizes existing reports and safes resources for your department.

Applying transformational management

So, how you can now apply these things? I also asked this myself. As I recognized those points, I asked myself how and where I should start to transform.

I thought about some skills respectively characteristics that I could firstly evaluate and influence afterwards. In order to do this I created an array. For getting started in the first place, I decided upon a subjective evaluation from my perspective. At the first step you can use grades for the evaluation. For reasons of simplification you can also use a scale from 0 to 10. With that you can calculate percentage results easily.

Loyalty – How does the employee see me? This is a very important question regarding transformational management.
Commitment – How committed is the employee to deliver a specific performance? With that we do not speak about the ability to perform but the motivation (The readiness to do something).

Responsibility – Is the employee ready to take responsibility for his own results?

Self-discipline – Is the employee ready to act entrepreneurial and to keep his targets in sight (and, of course, to pursue them)?

Team spirit – Is the employee ready to follow the weakest link in the chain and to support to the point that the team targets are fulfilled, anyway?

Learning receptivity – Up to what extent is the employee willing to break the mould to perform better and wanting it in the first place?

With these characteristics I created an array and evaluated intuitively on a scale of 1 to 10, whereby 10 was the best possible value.

Such a subjective evaluation is, of course, always something to scruple about. You also could link those valuations on specific things. Therefore, it is quite conceivable that the targets that were achieved so far, for example, could set off self-discipline. If the employee had to achieve 12 targets, which would comply with a year, these 12 targets yield 100 %.

If the employee has achieved 9 targets out of these 12 the rate of target achievement would be 75%. If you divide this percentage by 10 it'll result 7.5 points on our scale for self-discipline.

To get a quick overview of the current situation I chose the above-mentioned subjective evaluation. That means, I sat down and simply estimated the points.

The result was, as shown above, sobering. I didn't expect the average values of the single criteria to be beneath 8. At least I saw a great potential for transformation. It was even more important that I saw, where I should transform first. It clearly was the team spirit.

However, all of the other topics didn't come out as I expected them to. So, how can you now influence every single criteria respectively characteristics? That was my next step.

After further long researches and deliberations the following important indications arose as results:

Loyalty – develops from a model. The employee knows that his team manager respectively superior practices the tasks as good as he preaches them. Transparency leads to a mutual target. You cannot demand loyalty. It only develops from similarity. It also develops, as mentioned above, from common actions.

Commitment – also develops from a role model function and especially through inspiration (challenge). Small innuendos of their own successes could help to encourage the employees to do "it" even better.

Responsibility – develops through entrepreneurial behaviour (innovation). Transparency and enlightenment is also very important. Employees should see for themselves, which consequences are occurring from their actions. As a manager you also should keenly accept and promote improvement suggestions from your employees. Exactly those suggestions for optimizations are an indicator for entrepreneurial behaviour and thinking.

Self-discipline – develops through entrepreneurial behavior (innovation) and especially through competency development and fair communication. Achievement of objectives and engagement on their own professional career are strong indicators for self-discipline. To promote and to demand these things is an important task in this regard.

Team spirit – develops through fair communication and similarities. Negative feedbacks about single employees should not be made public within the team. As a manager you can emphasise the team performance. Team events or staff outings promote the community spirit and give space for discussions within the team.

It would be utopian to think that the colleagues would debate over the latest on such a team event. Usually all of them have just one thing in common: their work. So you should use this and promote the exchange.

Learning receptivity – develops through the stimulus to perform. Similar to the point commitment, innuendos of the employees own successes could be helpful. Comparisons could be even more helpful. According to the principle "Employee A has achieved this and that, because he completed this and that training, so you could accomplish this as well." The motivation to learn something can be influenced positively.

During my researches I've encountered the phrase "black-hatted-practices". This obviously means that transformational leadership is bad or unethical, because it is done intentionally. This means, you make people change on purpose. Certainly, ethic plays an important part in that regard.

In my opinion it bears no challenge to apply transformational leadership. After all, it is about how to handle tasks better and in some sort of way about a more contended way of working. If the tasks are handled best everyone has the rewards for it.
From this perspective it's a Win-Win situation.

Summary

You will be a successful manager by focusing on your employees. You have to encourage the employees and demand something from them. Rely on your team and support it whenever it is necessary. Make enough time for your team and plan a walk on a daily base. This walk brings you even more nearer to your team. You will hear and experience things you otherwise would not notice at all.

Be a friend and auxiliary in crises. Support wherever you can, but also set appropriate limits. Show that you are a manager. Reflect your team and yourself on a regular basis. Place your trust in your employees and involve them.

Good luck!

Moore books from Ronny Behr:

http://goo.gl/Xaai4w

http://amzn.to/2bxnRa5

Website of the author:
http://ronnybehr.de

www.ingramcontent.com/pod-product-compliance
Lightning Source LLC
Chambersburg PA
CBHW021445170526
45164CB00001B/399